MUSIC AND KEYBOARD IN THE CLASSROOM

Let's Get Creative!

MICHAEL GRIFFIN

Published by Music Education World

Adelaide, Australia

First Published 2013

Copyright © 2013 Michael Griffin

Design by Michael Griffin

All rights reserved.

ISBN-13: 978-1492977100
ISBN-10: 1492977101

Dedicated to general music teachers in the classroom, for opening young ears to the magic of music.

ALSO BY MICHAEL GRIFFIN

Learning Strategies for Musical Success
Bumblebee! Rounds & Warm-ups for Choirs
Modern Harmony Method
Developing Musical Skill- For Students
Children and Learning – For Parents

Enquiries: michael@professional-development.com.au

Professional-Development.com.au

CONTENTS

LESSON 1:	EXTENDING ODE TO JOY	9
MORE ABOUT CHORD SYMBOLS		11
LESSON 2:	SWAN LAKE	12
LESSON 3:	THE BLUE DANUBE	13
LESSON 4:	FRERE JACQUES	15
LESSON 5:	CAN-CAN	17
LESSON 6:	WHAT TUNE IS THIS?	19
LESSON 7:	C PENTATONIC	20
LESSON 8:	C PENTATONIC PART TWO	22
LESSON 9:	C PENTATONIC DUET	23
LESSON 10:	RHYTHMIC READING	24
LESSON 11:	BRAHMS LULLABY	25
LESSON 12:	CONTRARY MOTION	27
LESSON 13:	JAZZ DRUMS	29
LESSON 14:	JAZZ BASS	30
LESSON 15:	JAZZ DRUM & BASS DUO	31
LESSON 16:	JAZZ PIANO	32
LESSON 17:	JAZZ TRIO	33
LESSON 18:	MOONLIGHT SONATA	34
LESSON 19:	GREENSLEEVES	35
LESSON 20:	CHOPSTICKS	38
STUDENT REFLECTIONS		41
TEACHER COMMENTS		42
ABOUT THE AUTHOR		44

MUSIC AND KEYBOARD IN THE CLASSROOM

Notes for the Teacher

One of the features of this keyboard course is the unique evaluation method. Regular feedback is important to keep students engaged and challenged. Whilst students are working with headphones, the opportunity presents itself for the teacher to monitor each student and give immediate feedback. In the student book, you will notice that each lesson includes a requirement to be signed by both teacher and student:

This piece has been played successfully.

☐ **Student signature**……………………………….

Teacher signature……………………………….

Date………………………………..

Have students sign when they think they have played it correctly. Some students will be reticent to do this, wanting you to check it for them. But students must learn how to assess their level of musicianship. By self-assessment they gain confidence in their increasing competence. The process of comparing their own judgements with those of the teacher will move them closer to this goal of trusting their own judgement.

When the student has signed her work, the teacher can then listen to the exercise. If successful, the piece can be signed by the teacher and dated. If not satisfactory, just telling the student what is wrong with their playing without giving them an opportunity to discover it themselves deprives them of a learning opportunity. Creative questioning is a technique which leads to self-discovery of the problem. Help the student discover the errors. Another technique is to ask the student to think thoughts out aloud. This meta-cognitive process quickly gets to the source of problems. Once the student has signed an exercise, they proceed to the next exercise. Students do not require a teacher signature to move on. I tell students to trust their own judgement and they will be seen to shortly. This saves student time in waiting for the teacher to sign work and puts the responsibility on the student to make decisions regarding their progress. This is a differentiated course meaning that student's progress independently rather than at the same time.

A significant feature of the assessment process is:

I am not the only 'teacher' who can sign an exercise.

Students who play an exercise particularly well may be granted 'teacher' status for that exercise. This allows them to browse the class and assess others in the same way an adult teacher does. This is an essential and very motivating aspect of this course.

All students understand the following:

- Student 'teachers' are to be respected and treated like normal teachers. Students who don't respect this might not get an opportunity to become 'teachers'.
- Student 'teachers' may have their rights revoked if they are too lenient or too harsh in assessing student work

Students love this concept and take it seriously. This creates opportunities for higher level thinking and learning, and for the teacher to observe peer interaction. I aim to give every student the opportunity to be a student teacher and thus create opportunities for all students to develop student leadership and responsibility. But I only reward teacher status on merit; otherwise it becomes meaningless. Notice the box on the LHS of the signature lines. 'T' for teacher status can be written here. At the end of this book is a reflection page. Encourage students to write one reflection per lesson. For example:

I have mastered lesson 7. I'm pleased because it's been really difficult for me.
There's one section in lesson 8 I just can't get. I think I need to repeat it a lot.
Today, Jessie helped me with lesson 5. It makes more sense now.

Music and Keyboard in the Classroom aims to increase a personal level of musicianship through the practical activity of learning keyboard. It endeavors to develop creativity and to stir the imagination, and hopefully will contribute to fostering a lifelong love of making music and listening to music.
I hope you enjoy teaching this course.

Michael Griffin
August 2013.

Lesson 1:   Extending Ode to Joy

There are two differences between this version of *Ode to Joy* and the one learned in *Music and Keyboard: Fundamentals of Notation*.

Firstly, this one is in the key of F major, not C major. When we change key, the music is the same but in higher or lower *pitch*. There are a few reasons why we should want to change the key of music. One is that different keys suit different singers because people sing in different vocal ranges.

Second, this version is longer. The first two staves are the same, but the third stave is new. Note how the fourth stave is the same as the second. Music is based on repetition and contrast. Stave three contrasts the repetition of the other staves. To help understand the repetition and contrast within a piece, consider the design or structure, or *form*.

The form of this piece is represented as follows:

A   A'   B   A'

As staves one, two and four are the same or almost the same, we call this material A. Stave three is different, hence the new letter B. Staves two and four are exactly the same – A'.

This *ternary* form represents a design which has:

>Opening statement (sometimes repeated)
>
>Different statement
>
>Opening statement again

Notice the marking **mf** under the first note. This is called a *dynamic marking*. Dynamics indicate how loud or soft to play. **mf** is an Italian abbreviation for *mezzo forte*, or moderately loud.

MICHAEL GRIFFIN

This piece has been played successfully.

Student signature……………………………..

Teacher signature……………………………..

Date……………………………..

Questions

1. What is the key signature of F major?

2. Put in a suitable fingering for the B section below the notes.

3. Which Beethoven Symphony is this tune from?

4. How many symphonies did Beethoven write?

5. Define:

   a. transpose

   b. form

   c. ternary form

More about chord symbols

Now that you have a grasp of left hand notes and an ability to put two hands together, it's time to explore playing with chords. Many keyboards have an inbuilt accompaniment system where by pressing one or more notes in the left hand, a full rhythm section of bass guitar, guitar, strings and drums supports the melody that you play with your right hand. This will be easier to understand if someone shows you how to do this. It's not difficult, but you will need to practise the co-ordination.

The **first** step is to experiment with the keyboard accompaniment system. That alone will be a lot of fun!

The **second** step is to go back to earlier exercises. Work in pairs: you play the chords whilst your partner plays the melody. Then swap so you both get the practice required to improve. There are eight lessons in this book that use chord symbols. Practise all eight with a partner.

The **third** step is to play both the melody and the left hand accompaniment yourself. You will need to practise slowly, only gradually increasing the tempo. Note that lessons 9 and 19 are already for two hands, so you will need to either adjust the melody or stick to playing these as duets.

Chords can also be played on instruments such as guitars, and bass guitars play the single 'name' note of a chord. Find other musicians and start your band.

Lesson 2:   Swan Lake

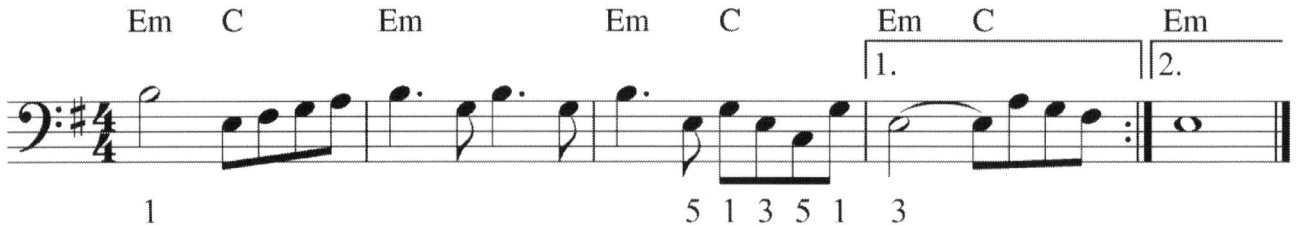

This piece has been played successfully with the left hand.

                               Student signature……………………………………..

                               Teacher signature……………………………………..

                                              Date……………………………………...

Questions

1. Name the key *(hint: consider the final note as well as the key signature)*.

2. Including the repeat, how many bars (measures) in this melody?

3. *Swan Lake* is one of the world's best loved ballets. Describe the story with a one paragraph synopsis.

Lesson 3: The Blue Danube

The Blue Danube has a time signature of three crotchet beats per bar. However, observe that the first bar has only one crotchet beat, and the final bar has two crotchet beats. This is not unusual. Many pieces begin with an incomplete bar so as to start on a weak beat rather than a strong beat. This is called an *anacrusis*. Here, beats in the last bar are added to the first, giving the correct number of beats per bar.

An anacrusis bar is not the first bar of music. Bar one is the first *full* bar of music. You will understand this by observing the bar numbers of *The Blue Danube*.

Research project: Johann Strauss

a. Photo

b. Birth/death dates

c. The names and musical examples of two other famous pieces besides *The Blue Danube*

d. The city and country where he lived

e. Find out about the *Blue Danube*

f. Play the orchestral version of this music and learn how to dance a waltz!

Questions

1. Name another piece you have played in simple triple time.

2. Name the notes in bars 11-14 inclusive.

If music be the food of love, play on. - *Shakespeare*

This curved line is called a *tie*. A tie joins two notes together and the second note is held but not played.

Therefore in this example the dotted minim C is tied to the minim C. Hence, C is held for 3+2= 5 counts.

This piece has been played successfully with the left hand.

Student signature……………………………………

Teacher signature……………………………………

Date…………………………………..

MUSIC AND KEYBOARD IN THE CLASSROOM

Lesson 4: Frere Jacques

This French round requires groups of four. Play it yourself before trying it in a group.

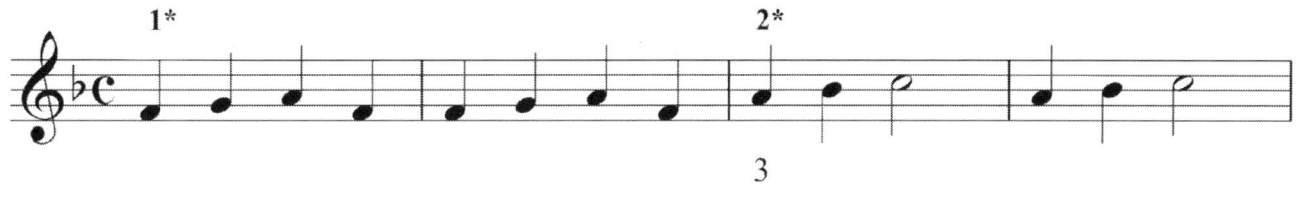

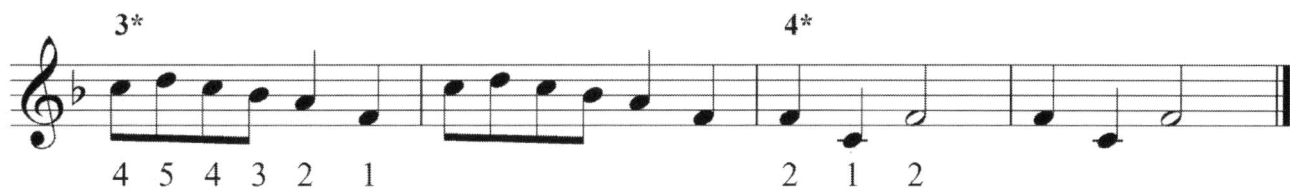

This piece has been played successfully as a solo.

☐
                               Student signature…………………………………

                               Teacher signature…………………………………

                               Date…………………………………

This piece has been played successfully in ensemble.

☐
                               Student signature…………………………………

                               Teacher signature…………………………………

                               Date…………………………………

Activities

1. Find the words in French and English for *Frere Jacques*.

    <u>French</u>   <u>English</u>

2. Sing *Frere Jacques* as a round in a group of four.

3. What other rounds do you know? List them here.

MUSIC AND KEYBOARD IN THE CLASSROOM

Lesson 5: Can-Can

Composers often repeat sections of music. Repeat signs avoid having to write out the same passage again.

:|| This repeat sign in *Can-Can* occurs in bar four (at the end of the first time bar). On reaching this point, go back to the beginning and play the first three bars again. Skip the first time bar and finish with the second time bar.

On the top LHS of the music is the metronome marking ♩ = 110.

This indicates that a suitable performing tempo would be at 110 beats per minute. Use the metronome function on the keyboard. Practice slowly and gradually work up to this tempo, as mistakes practised are difficult to remove.

If this tempo is too fast for you (or too slow!) you can write in your new tempo at the top L.H side of the music.

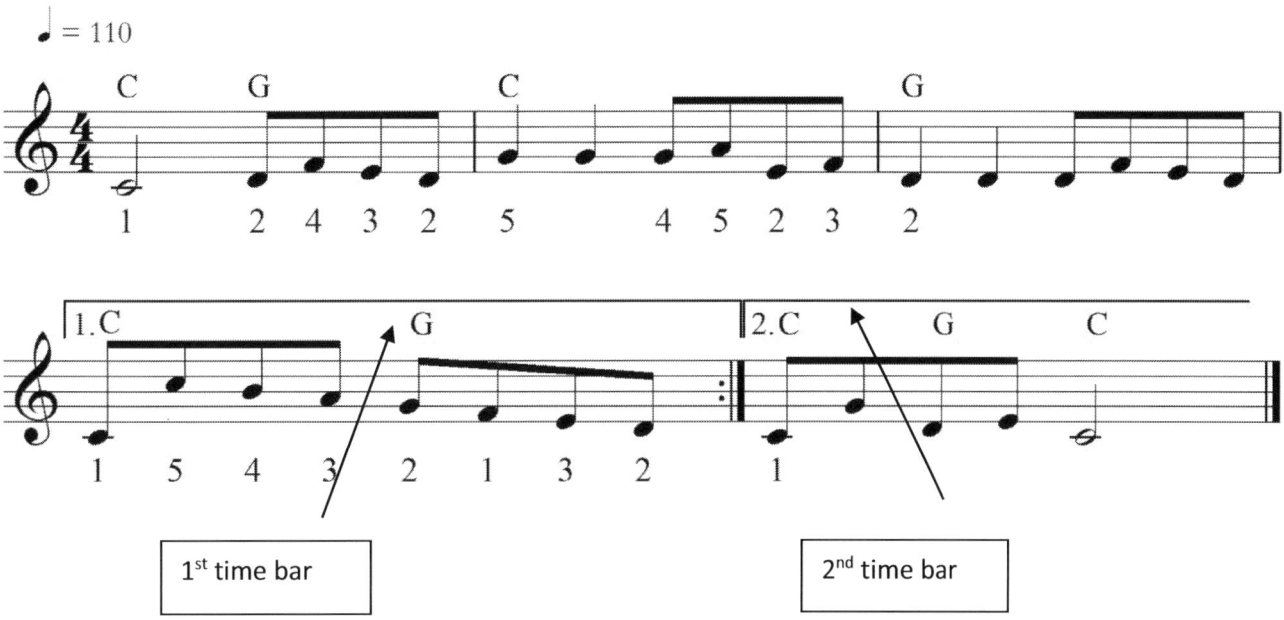

This piece has been played successfully at the tempo ♩ = _____

Student signature…………………………………..

Teacher signature…………………………………..

Date……………………………………..

Questions

1. Including the repeat sign, what is the total number of bars played in *Can-Can*?

2. Who invented the metronome?

3. Visit http://www.metronomeonline.com and experiment with this online metronome. Metronome applications are also available for smart phones.

4. If a metronome marking was ♩ = **120**, then

a) How many beats per minute is this?

b) How many beats per second?

Research project: Jacques Offenbach and the *Can-Can*

a. Describe the *Can-Can*.

b. When and in which country was it famous?

c. What is the *Moulin Rouge*?

d. Which work of Jacques Offenbach did *Can-Can* come from?

e. Listen to the orchestrated version of this music. How would you describe it?

MUSIC AND KEYBOARD IN THE CLASSROOM

Lesson 6: What tune is this?

_____

Can you work out what tune this is? Write in the missing notes and name the tune on the line above. The value of the missing note is written above the stave.

This piece has been played successfully.

☐   **Student signature**……………………………………

                               Teacher signature……………………………………

                               Date……………………………………

Questions

1. What central note is this piece is based around? ………………………..

2. What is the name of the two numbers before the first note? ………………………..

Lesson 7: C Pentatonic

Improvisation is something we do every day in conversation with others. Often, we don't plan our responses, we respond naturally in line with the topic of conversation. Similarly, musicians like to improvise using scales and chords as a basis or 'topic' of musical conversation. In this lesson, you will improvise on C major pentatonic over a two-chord ostinato figure.

The major pentatonic scale has two less notes than the seven-note major scale. Here is the C major scale:

C D E [F] G A [B]

The boxed notes are the ones we omit - notes on the 4th and 7th scale degrees. Therefore, from any major scale, a pentatonic scale can be built from the scale degrees 1 2 3 5 6. Hence C pentatonic:

C D E   G A
1 2 3   5 6

The first 3 bars of the exercise below give you the opportunity to practise this new scale. Play it several times and get used to excluding the F and B. The rest of the music is an example improvisation made up from crotchets and quavers. Learn how to play this before trying your own improvisation.

This piece has been played successfully.

☐　　　　　　　　　　　　Student signature……………………………..

　　　　　　　　　　　　　Teacher signature……………………………..

　　　　　　　　　　　　　　　　　　Date………………………….....

Lots of songs have been written using the pentatonic scale.

Here are some pentatonic songs you might know. If not, look them up – they are great songs to learn!

- All Night, All Day
- Amazing Grace
- Bought Me A Cat
- Camptown Races
- Ezekiel Saw The Wheel
- Get On Board (Little Children)
- Mull Of Kintrye
- Sakura
- Skye Boat Song
- Swing Low Sweet Chariot
- This Train (Is Bound For Glory)
- Who Built The Ark?

Learn to play a pentatonic song from this list – or find one of your own.

MICHAEL GRIFFIN

Lesson 8: C Pentatonic Part Two

This is an accompaniment for the previous exercise. Bar one consists of notes form the chord C major 7, and bar two notes from the chord F major 7. Above each bar is a chord symbol.

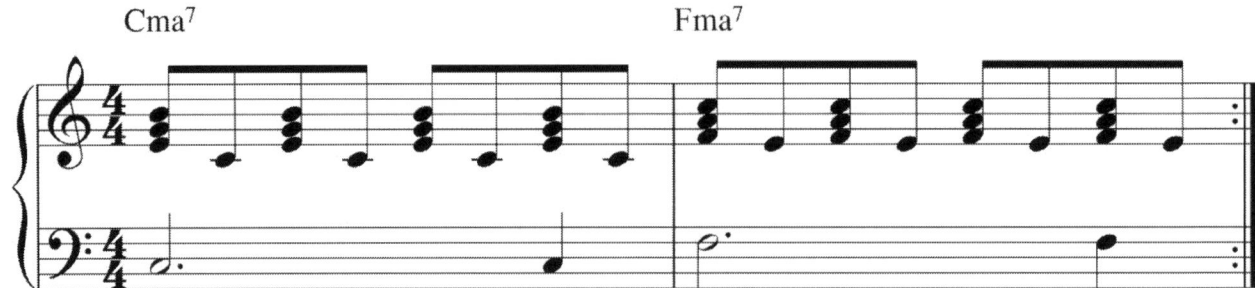

This accompaniment has been played successfully.

Student signature………………………………..

Teacher signature………………………………..

Date………………………………..

Lesson 9: C Pentatonic Duet

Team up with a partner. Player Two starts the accompaniment pattern from lesson 8 and after a short introduction – perhaps 2 or 4 bars, the 'improviser' enters and makes up little melodies using the C major pentatonic from lesson 7. Here are some suggestions:

- Start by playing the written improvisation in lesson 7.
- Avoid always starting a phrase on C
- Hold some long notes
- Give your phrases plenty of space
- Work hard to keep in time with your accompanist

The accompanist plays the two-bar ostinato continually until Player One indicates to finish. Finish on a C major 7 chord. You have to work really hard to keep in time with your partner. This is called *ensemble work*. Have fun! There are no right or wrong answers. It takes some courage to improvise but gradually you will find your own expressive voice.

Here is an alternative to playing this as a duet. Many modern keyboards have *record* functions as well as automatic accompaniment functions. If your keyboard allows, record the accompaniment many times over, perhaps ten, and on playback practise your improvisation. Another option is to use the auto-accompaniment on a style such as *ballad*. If you can do this with your left hand, your right hand will be free to improvise. This is easier than it probably sounds, but have someone show you how it works. Experiment with the automatic accompaniment function. It's a lot of fun and includes introductions, style changes, drum fills and endings. You can be the whole band all be yourself!

This duet has been played successfully.

Student signature……………………………..

Teacher signature……………………………..

Date……………………………..

MICHAEL GRIFFIN

Lesson 10: Rhythmic Reading

Continue to write the pulse underneath the rhythm of *Lullaby,* below. Then apply these four rhythmic learning activities:

1. Clap the rhythm whilst counting the pulse out loud.

2. Clap the pulse and sing the rhythm. Choose a sound such as 'doo', 'da', 'loo', 'la', or 'koo', 'kah'.

3. Left hand pulse, right hand rhythm

4. Right hand pulse, left hand rhythm

'Clap the rhythm whilst counting the pulse out loud' has been performed successfully.

Student signature……………………………..

Teacher signature……………………………

Date……………………………

MUSIC AND KEYBOARD IN THE CLASSROOM

Lesson 11: Brahms Lullaby

Now you are ready to learn the Brahms Lullaby. But first, look at the rhythm and notice this unit of music.

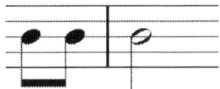

This is called a *motif*, a defining element of a piece. This short-short-long motif is prominent in *Lullaby*.

This piece has been played successfully.

                                    Student signature…………………………………..

                                    Teacher signature…………………………………..

                                                Date…………………………………..

Questions

1. How many bars in *Lullaby*?

2. Explain the key signature.

3. What is the time signature? Explain the number of beats per bar and the type of beat. What is the accent distribution in terms of strong, medium and weak of this meter?

4. Name the notes in bars 6 and 7.

5. Explain ♩ = 90 mean?

6. A lullaby is a soothing song sung to infants to help them sleep. How many lullabies do you know? List them here.

Lesson 12: Contrary Motion

MICHAEL GRIFFIN

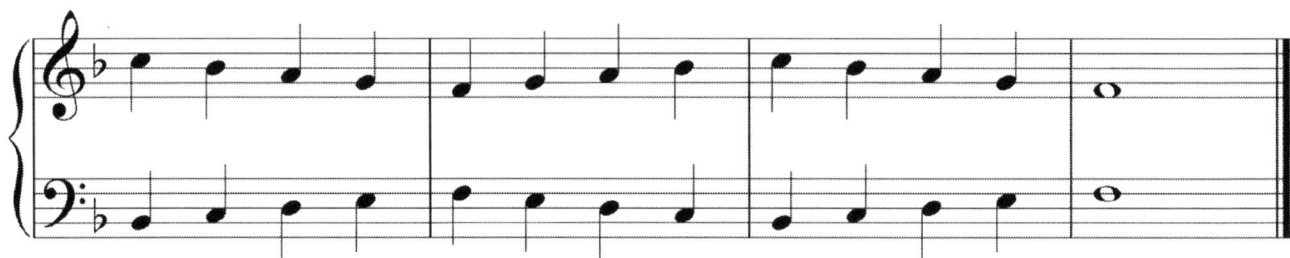

These three scales have been played successfully.

                              Student signature……………………………….

                              Teacher signature……………………………….

                              Date……………………………….

Questions

1. Why are some notes shaded?

2. What is the key signature of F major?

3. Name the relative minor of F major? (Hint: count up to the 6th note of the F major scale)

4. Why are scales useful for learning to play the keyboard?

MUSIC AND KEYBOARD IN THE CLASSROOM

Lesson 13:   Jazz Drums

For this exercise select a *Jazz Kit* setting if your keyboard has one. Otherwise leave it as is.

The drum pattern below is played with three different sounds; bass, snare and hi-hat. Find where these sounds are within the *Jazz Kit* setting of the keyboard and use the same procedure as lesson 15 to learn this.

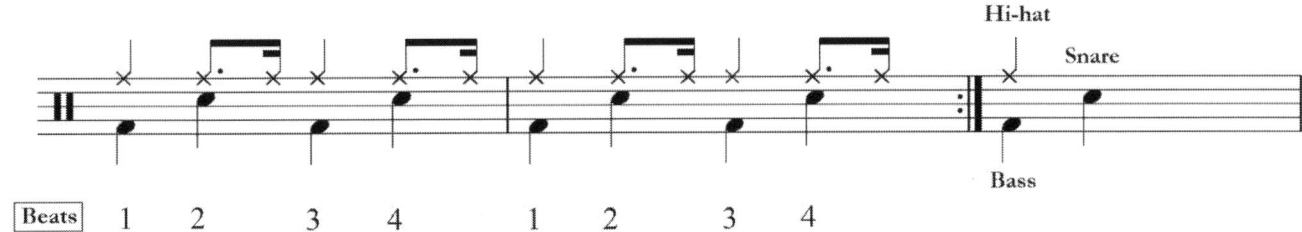

Advice

- The bass drum is played on beats 1 and 3. Play this whilst counting the four-beat pulse.

- The snare drum is played on beats 2 and 4. Play this whilst counting the four-beat pulse.

- Combine bass and snare using two fingers of your left hand. Count aloud as you do this.

- Play the hi-hat figure with your right hand whilst counting the four-beat pulse.

- Combine the bass drum and hi-hat, then the snare drum and hi-hat, and eventually all three instruments of the drum kit.

Use a practice partner(s) playing different parts of the drum kit.

This piece has been played successfully.

Student signature……………………………………

Teacher signature……………………………………

Date……………………………………

Lesson 14:   **Jazz Bass**

Select a *jazz bass* sound on your keyboard. It can be fretless or acoustic, and many keyboard brands store these sounds in numbers 41 or 43.

The exercise consists of five two-bar jazz bass patterns. Typically, an experienced bass player varies patterns like these to keep a bass line interesting.

Each two-bar pattern has a repeat sign, so play it many times to get comfortable with it. When you are ready to sign, play at a moderate tempo without stopping and without the repeats.

This is to be played with the left hand. If you think the sound of the bass is either too low of too high, play it in another *register*. This means the same set of notes up or down an octave.

This piece has been played successfully with the left hand.

Student signature…………………………………..

Teacher signature…………………………………..

Date…………………………………..

Lesson 15: Jazz Drums & Bass Duo

Now that you can play jazz drums and jazz bass, it is time to play a duet. With a partner, one person plays bass lines and the other plays the jazz-drum pattern. Use the metronome to keep in time, and swap roles when you have mastered your part. In lesson 17, the drums and bass will form a *rhythm section* with the piano.

As discussed in lesson 9, you might record one part and practise the other, eliminating the need for a partner.

This ensemble has been played in time.

Student signature……………………………………..

Teacher signature……………………………………..

Date……………………………………..

Question

Louis Armstrong, Duke Ellington and Miles Davis are three all-time greats in jazz music. Can you name five more jazz legends?

1.
2.
3.
4.
5.

MICHAEL GRIFFIN

Lesson 16:   Jazz Piano

Add the piano part to bass and drums, to form a *trio*. These chords are based on the *dorian* scale, a type of minor scale common in jazz.

Some notes on the top stave have a dot underneath. This is called *staccato* and means to play the note in a short and detached manner. When you play staccato it should feel like touching a hot plate, as you need to withdraw your finger quickly. The other marking - a **v** lying on its side, is called an *accent*. Accented notes get a louder than usual attack. Both staccato and accented notes are types of *articulation*, referring to how a note should be played. In music it is not only playing the right note counts but playing the right articulation and volume levels as well.

This rhythm looks difficult because some notes are played off the beat. This is a feature of jazz called *syncopation* and helps to make it sound 'cool'. The rhythms can be difficult to read, so learn by copying the teacher, then practise with a metronome. Each chord has three notes played simultaneously. Fingers 1, 3 and 5 of the right hand will handle these chords comfortably, so the fingering need not change.

This chordal figure has been played successfully with the metronome.

                                      Student signature..

                                      Teacher signature..

                                                  Date..

Lesson 17: Jazz Trio

Now you can play jazz drums, jazz bass, and jazz piano chords, it is time to form a jazz trio. Make sure that you swap roles to give each member of the trio an opportunity to experience each instrument.

This jazz trio rhythm section has played accurately and in time.

☐

Student signature......................................

Teacher signature......................................

Date......................................

Now that you have played jazz drums, bass and piano, which instrument did you find easiest? List them in order of difficulty from easiest to hardest.

1.

2.

3.

MICHAEL GRIFFIN

Lesson 18:   Moonlight Sonata

This piece has been played successfully.

☐

Student signature……………………………………..

Teacher signature……………………………………..

Date……………………………………..

Questions

1. Write the composer's name at the top RHS of the music.

2. Write a suggested *tempo* indication at the top LHS of the music. It is traditional to use an Italian term.

3. Note the repetitive three-note broken chords throughout the music. What is the name for broken chords?

4. This music is but a small section of the whole piano sonata that totals about 18 minutes. How many piano sonatas did this composer write?

Lesson 19:   Greensleeves

This popular English folk song was written about 1580. It is also the tune of the Christmas carol _____.

To learn this, practise in small 'chunks' and pay particular attention to the fingering. As the old English saying goes - *an ounce of preparation is worth a pound of cure*. Longer pieces of music usually take several practise sittings to achieve a level of fluency, so aim to learn just a little more each day. With difficult pieces of keyboard music it is a good idea to learn with separate hands. This is best done slowly with lots of repetition, but remember that every time you repeat a mistake you learn that mistake, so practise it the right way as soon as possible. Another good learning technique is to practise the left hand by itself, whilst humming the tune. You can also play this with a partner, taking one hand each.

A piece of music will usually consist of repeated phrases. In *Greensleeves* for example, bars 1-4 occur again as bars 9-12. Can you find other occurrences of repetition? Bars 25-28 are almost an exact copy of which bars? _____.

By identifying repetition within a piece we realise that there is less to be learned than first thought.

MICHAEL GRIFFIN

Greensleeves has been played successfully.

☐   **Student signature**………………………………..

                             Teacher signature………………………………..

                                         Date…………………………………..

Questions

1. What is the key of this piece?

2. What do we call a sharp or a flat that is in the music, but not in the key signature?

3. Google the painting 'My Lady Greensleeves' in the 1864 painting by Dante Gabriel Rossetti. Do you like it?

Lesson 20:   Chopsticks

Chopsticks is a piano duet. It can be played with both players on one keyboard, or with two separate keyboards.

Player Two is played with both hands and is the easier part. Note that this is an accompaniment, and is a repeated four-bar pattern. A repeated pattern like this is called an *ostinato*. Use the suggested fingering, and when you think you know it, play it with your eyes closed to improve your feel for the keyboard.

This accompaniment has been played successfully with eyes closed!

Student signature………………………………….

Teacher signature………………………………….

Date………………………………….

Many melodies have been composed to fit the *Chopsticks* accompaniment. Parts A, B and C below represent three of these. Part A is the most common and is sometimes played with both hands. However if you aspire to play *Chopsticks* as a soloist, you need to be able to play this melody with your right hand only. Part B is a major scale pattern descending on the white notes. The 16 bars are essentially an 8-bar pattern repeated. Pattern C is also an 8-bar pattern repeated, but is more chromatic in nature, having accidentals.

This version of Chopsticks ends with the A section, making it quite a long piece.

These sections have been played successfully (circle)　　A　　　　B　　　　C

Student signature…………………………………

Teacher signature…………………………………

Date…………………………………

Questions

1. Name the two accidentals in section C of the melody.

2. Played right through as written, how many bars long is this piece?

3. Define:

    a) Ostinato

    b) Chromatic

Did you know? 'Chopstick's original name was 'The Celebrated Chop Waltz'. There are wonderful virtuosic versions of 'Chopsticks' on YouTube. Explore! What is your favourite?

Student reflections

This page is to record moments when you are pleased with your achievement and progress, or when you get frustrated. Recalling how you worked to overcome difficulties will enhance the likelihood of future success.

Date	Comment

Teacher comments

This page is for the teacher to record when pleased with the way you are working, and also when there is some advice or practice technique to help you.

Date	Comment

Congratulations!

You have completed

MUSIC AND KEYBOARD IN THE CLASSROOM

Let's Get Creative!

ABOUT THE AUTHOR

An Australian citizen who has taught and consulted throughout the world, Michael Griffin is a pianist, conductor, educator and author. Griffin has been the Keynote or Consultant Speaker at numerous global education events in more than 30 countries He has been an invited guest at the New Horizons adult education program in Rochester NY, and has consulted for Cambridge University Press designing music education curriculum for Kazakhstan. As a conductor, his school ensembles have received numerous awards, including the Australasian Open Choral Championship. Griffin is a recipient of the South Australian Education and Arts Ministers' Prize and is listed in the Who's Who South Australia. Besides *Music and Keyboard in the Classroom,* Griffin is the author of *Learning Strategies for Musical Success, Developing Musical Skill – for Students, Modern Harmony Method: Fundamentals of Jazz and Popular Harmony, Bumblebee! Rounds and Warm-ups for Choirs,* and *Children and Learning – For Parents.* As a pianist, Griffin has held guest residencies at Dubai's Burj al Arab and Australia's Hayman Island, and recorded two CD's of classical piano. His website is Professional-Development.com.au.

Printed in Poland
by Amazon Fulfillment
Poland Sp. z o.o., Wrocław